AF449060

PABLO PICASSO'S CONFUSING ART

ART HISTORY TEXTBOOK

Children's Art, Music & Photography Books

Pablo Picasso was an artist born in Spain on October 25, 1881 and died in France on April 8, 1973. Some of his famous modern works of art are *The Weeping Woman, Guernica, Three Musicians* and *The Pipes of Pan.* In this book, you will learn about his life and his style of art.

A waxwork of Pablo Picasso.

PICASSO'S
EARLY LIFE

Pablo Picasso grew up in Spain. He was baptized with the name of Pablo Diego José Francisco de Paula Juan Nepomuceno María de los Remedios Cipriano de la Santísima Trinidad Ruiz y Picasso, a succession of names honoring numerous relatives and saints. He knew he liked to draw at an early age.

Legend says that one of his first words was *"piz"*, which is short for *"pencil"* in Spanish. Soon, it became apparent that he was a very talented artist, but had very little interest in school. He began receiving formal artistic training at the age of 7 from his father in oil painting and figure drawing.

His father was a traditional style academic instructor and artist and believe proper training needed disciplined replication of the masters, and sketching the human body from live models and plaster casts. His son soon became preoccupied with art to the detriment of his school work.

He attended a well-known art school located in Barcelona at the age of 14. He then went to a different school in Madrid a few years later. He soon became bored with the art school's classic teachings. He did not like painting similarly to how people had painted for hundreds of years in the past. He wanted to create a new style of art.

In 1891, they moved to A Coruña, and his father started working as a professor at the School of Fine Arts. They lived there about four years. Pablo's father once found Pablo painting over the sketch of a pigeon that was not yet finished.

Noting his son's techniques and precision, Ruiz knew that his 13-year-old son was better than he and decided to give up his painting, although his paintings existed in later years.

Picasso's seven-year-old sister, Conchita, died in 1895 from diphtheria and he was traumatized by this. His family then moved to Barcelona, and Ruiz started classes at the local School of Fine Arts.

Picasso loved the city and felt that it was his true home in times of nostalgia or sadness. His father was able to persuade the academy officials to permit Pablo to take an exam for an advanced class. While this process would often take students a month to complete, he was able to complete it in a week. At the young age of 13, he was admitted.

He lacked discipline but made friends that would affect him during his later life. Ruiz then rented a small room for him which was close to home so he could be alone to work, yet he checked up on him many times during the day to check out his drawings. They would have frequent arguments.

Picasso's uncle and father decided they wanted to send him to Madrid's Real Academia de Bellas Artes de San Fernando, which was the country's best School of Art. At 16, he set off on his own for the first time, but didn't like formal instruction and quit going to classes right after his enrollment. Madrid had several different attractions.

The Prado had paintings created by Diego Velázquez, Francisco Zurbarán and Francisco Goya. He particularly liked the artistry of El Greco; the elements of arresting color, elongated limbs and mystical visages, which elements are echoed in his later works of art.

Modigliani, Picasso and André Salmon in front the Café de la Rotonde, Paris.

BLUE
PERIOD

From 1901 to 1904, known as his Blue Period, his paintings were characterized as somber and they were rendered in varying shades of blue and blue green, occasionally being warmed with other colors. Several paintings of gaunt mothers with children were dated from this period. He divided time during this period between Paris and Barcelona.

His austere use of color and occasionally sad subjects - beggars and prostitutes often his subjects - was influenced by a trip around Spain and the suicide of his close friend, Carlos Casagemas.

Beginning the autumn of 1901 he painted many posthumous portraits of Casagemas, which culminated in a gloomy allegorical painting in 1903, titled La Vie, which is now at the Cleveland Museum of Art.

This same blue mood suffuses the popular etching titled The Frugal Repast (1904), depicting a sighted woman and blind man, both of which are emaciated, sitting at an almost bare table.

Blindness occurs in a lot of his works during this time period, as represented in The Blindman's Meal (1903, Metropolitan Museum of Art) as well as in the portrait titled Celestina (1903).

Pablo Picasso, Moïse Kisling and Paquerette enjoying themselves at café La Rotonde, 1916.

ROSE PERIOD
(1904 - 1906)

The time between 1904 and 1906 was known as the Rose Period and was characterized by a cheerier style using orange and pink colors, featuring several circus people, harlequins and acrobats, which were known in France as saltimbanques. The harlequin, was a comedic character and typically depicted in a checkered pattern clothing which became Picasso's symbol. He then met Fernande Olivier in Paris, who was a bohemian artist and became his mistress in 1904.

She appears in several of his Rose Period works of art, many influenced by the warm relationship he had with her, as well as his increased exposure to French painting. The typically optimistic and upbeat mood of his paintings during this time period was reminiscent of the period between 1899 and 1901, just prior to his blue period, and 1904 was considered to be a transition year between the Blue Period and the Rose Period.

Acrobate et jeune Arlequin (Acrobat and Young Harlequin), 1905.

By 1905 Picasso became a favorite of American art collectors Gertrude and Leo Stein by 1905. Michael Stein, who was their older brother, along with Sarah, his wife, started collecting his work. He painted the portraits of Gertrude Stein and Allan Stein, her nephew.

Gertrude became his principal patron, acquiring his paintings and drawings and placing them on exhibit at her informal Salon which was at her house in Paris. He met Henri Matisse in 1905 at one of her gatherings, and he became a rival and lifelong friend.

They also introduced him to Claribel Cone and Etta, her sister, who were collectors of American art, and they too starting acquiring Matisse's and Picasso's paintings. Leo Stein would eventually move to Italy. Sarah and Michael Stein became fans of Matisse, and Gertrude continued to collect Picasso's paintings.

Lady with a Fan, 1905 by Pablo Picasso, oil on canvas

Daniel-Henry Kahnweiler by Picasso, 1910.

CUBISM
(1907 - 1921)

Picasso started experimenting with a new and different style of painting in 1907. He teamed up with Georges Braque, another artist. They had created a totally new style of painting by 1909 known as Cubism. With Cubism, the subjects are studied and broken into different sections. The sections are then placed back together and painted different angles and perspectives.

He started combining Cubism and collage in 1912. He used plaster or sand in the paint, giving it texture. He also applied materials such as newspapers, wallpaper, and colored paper to his paintings for added dimension.

Three Musicians and Ambroise Vollard are two examples of his Cubism paintings.

The Musee Picasso Museum, located in the Hotel Sale, Marais, Paris.

PIC
SSO
En raison de la préparation de l'exposition ¡ Picasso ! L'exposition anniversaire, aucune exposition n'est visible au niveau -1.
Due to the preparation of the exhibition ¡ Picasso ! L'exposition anniversaire, there is no exhibition at the level -1.

HIS NEOCLASSICAL STYLE

While he continued experimenting with Cubism, sometime around 1921 he went through a time period where he painted more classical type paintings. Picasso borrowed ideas from painters of the Renaissance, like Raphael. He created characters that were powerful and appeared to be somewhat three-dimensional, like a statue. *The Pipes of Pan* and *Woman in White* are examples of his works done in this style.

Picasso's Woman in White, 1923.

Guernica by Pablo Picasso

SURREALISM

Pablo became interested in Surrealism artwork around 1924. These types of paintings were not supposed to make any sense and often appeared to be something you might vision in a nightmare or dream. Even though he did not become a member of this movement, he incorporated some of the ideas into his work. Sometimes this time period is referred to as his Monster period. *Guernica* and *The Red Armchair* are examples of his paintings that have a surrealism influence.

The Red Armchair by Picasso, 1931.

Sculpture in Chicago by Picasso, USA.

LEGACY

Today, he is known as one of the best artists of the 20th century, and is considered by many to be one of the greatest artists in the history of art. He painted using many different styles and created several unique contributions to the art world. He painted several self-portraits towards the end of his life.

One of his last pieces was a self-portrait done on paper using crayon and titled Self-Portrait Facing Death. He passed away on April 8, 1973, one year later, at the age of 91.

Pablo Picasso was a great artist, even though a lot of people find it difficult to understand his work. Be sure to check it out yourself and form your own opinion.

For additional information about Picasso and his life you can go to your local library, research the internet, and ask questions of your teachers, family and friends.

Visit
BABY PROFESSOR
EDUCATION KIDS
www.BabyProfessorBooks.com
to download Free Baby Professor eBooks
and view our catalog of new and exciting
Children's Books